W
HODDER
Wayland

A LOOK AT LIFE IN

The Seventies

R. G. Grant

First published in Great Britain in
1999 by Wayland (Publishers) Ltd
Reprinted in 2000 by Hodder Wayland,
an imprint of Hodder Children's Books

Hodder Children's Books, a division of
Hodder Headline Ltd
338 Euston Road, London NW1 3BH

This book was prepared for Wayland Publishers Ltd
by Ruth Nason.

Series editor: Alex Woolf
Series design: Stonecastle Graphics/Carole Design
Book design: Ruth Nason

British Library Cataloguing in Publication Data

Grant, R. G.
    A look at life in the seventies
    1.History, Modern - 20th century - Juvenile
    literature
    2.Nineteen seventies - Juvenile literature
    I.Title II.Seventies
    909.8'27

ISBN 0 7502 2468 1

Printed and bound in Italy by G. Canale & C.S.p.A.,
Turin

Cover photographs

Top left: Olga Korbut (Camera Press)

Top right: The Sydney Opera House
(Topham Picturepoint)

Centre: John Travolta in *Saturday Night
Fever* (Paramount, courtesy Kobal)

Bottom left: Women marchers,
Washington, DC, 1971 (Camera Press)

Bottom right: Punks in the King's Road,
London (Topham Picturepoint)

Acknowledgements

The Author and Publishers thank the following
for their permission to reproduce photographs:
Bridgeman Art Library (private collection), page
28t; Camera Press: pages 10t, 17b, 19t, 26,
32-33, 36, 37t, 37b, 39b; Columbia (courtesy
Kobal): pages 39t, 40t; Hulton Getty: pages 5b, 6t,
9t, 10b, 11, 15, 17t, 18b, 19b, 20t, 21, 22t, 29,
30r, 32t, 34b; MGM (courtesy Kobal): page 20b;
Popperfoto: pages 4, 5t, 6b, 7b, 8t, 8b, 9b, 24t, 33,
34-35, 38t, 41; Retna Pictures: pages 22b, 23b,
24b, 25, 27t, 27b; Science Photo Library: pages 12,
13t, 13b, 14t, 14b, 16t; Telegraph Colour Library:
page 28b; Topham Picturepoint: pages 7t, 16b, 18t,
23t, 30t, 31, 35b, 40b; United Artists (courtesy
Kobal): page 38b.

Contents

A Look at...

...in the '70s

A LOOK AT THE NEWS IN THE '70s

The 1970s was a time when many people campaigned against the prejudices of the past. The drive for 'liberation' that had begun in the 1960s was still going on. But it was also a time of terrorist outrages and economic difficulties.

In 1971, the President of NBC News expressed concern about the introduction of women news readers:

'Audiences are less prepared to accept news from a woman's voice than a man's.'

Women's Lib

The most important protest movement of the 1970s was Women's Liberation. Women fought for an equal right to jobs and to promotion, and for equal pay when they did the same work as men. Militants protested against beauty contests and pin-up photos that showed women as 'sex objects' who were to be judged by their looks alone. And they demanded that men should do an equal share of housework and other chores.

◁ *Women's Lib marchers in 1971 protest against 'female oppression', of which they are carrying symbols.*

The United Nations declared the first International Women's Year in 1975. In many countries, new laws made it illegal to discriminate against women in education or work. Individual women achieved positions of power in a man's world, notably Margaret Thatcher, who became Britain's first woman prime minister in 1979.

Minority rights

Minorities everywhere were seeking equal rights and greater freedom. The Gay Liberation movement took off in the USA, demanding an end to prejudice and discrimination. In many parts of the world, native peoples began to demand more respect for their cultures and the return of stolen land.

In 1976, the Inuit of Canada laid claim to one fifth of the country's land area. In Australia, aborigines were given the vote for the first time in 1973. In the USA, Native Americans organized headline-grabbing protests.

African Americans continued to fight for equal treatment. There was significant progress. For example, Jimmy Carter, US president from 1977 to 1980, appointed an African American, Andrew Young, as US ambassador to the United Nations. By the end of the decade, about one in ten federal judges was an African American. But in general, blacks were still at the bottom of the social pile. 'Affirmative action' was introduced – the policy of encouraging firms to have 'quotas' of employees from minorities, including African Americans. And in 1971, the US Supreme Court approved the controversial policy of bussing black pupils to white schools to end racial segregation in education.

...Newsflash...

Wounded Knee, 8 May 1973. Armed militants of the American Indian Movement today ended their occupation of the Sioux reservation at Wounded Knee, South Dakota. The militants had been under siege inside the reservation, surrounded by FBI agents, for two months. They are demanding a public inquiry into the ill-treatment of Native Americans by the federal government. Wounded Knee was the site of a notorious massacre of Sioux by US cavalry in 1890. This time, despite exchanges of gunfire, a bloodbath was avoided.

◁ *Wounded Knee, 1973. Native Americans and US government officials walk around the teepee before going inside to discuss a settlement of the situation.*

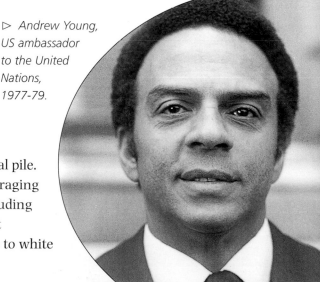

▷ *Andrew Young, US ambassador to the United Nations, 1977-79.*

Bad times for the USA

The 1970s was a bad time for the USA's international power and prestige. The presidency was shaken by the Watergate scandal. An investigation by journalists on the *Washington Post* revealed that officials in the White House had been behind a burglary of the Democratic Party head-quarters in the Watergate building in 1972. President Richard M. Nixon was implicated in covering up this crime and was forced to resign in 1974.

Abroad, there were many setbacks for the USA. In Africa, pro-communist governments backed by Cuba and the

Soviet Union came to power in Ethiopia, Angola and Mozambique. In Central America, the Sandinista revolution in 1979 over-threw a US-backed military regime in Nicaragua and brought a left-wing government into the USA's backyard. In the same year, in Iran, the rule of Shah Reza Pahlavi was ended by mass popular uprising. The country's new ruler, the Islamic fundamentalist Ayatollah Khomeini, denounced the USA as the 'Great Satan', and allowed revolutionary students to take Americans from the US embassy hostage.

◁ *Supporters of Ayatollah Khomeini, Tehran, 1979.*

Profile

Richard M. Nixon

Richard Milhous Nixon was a clever but sometimes devious Republican politician. US President from 1968, he was re-elected in 1972, but soon ran into difficulties. His attempts to block investigation of the Watergate scandal were uncovered during public hearings in Congress. During these hearings, tapes were played of the president's conversations in the White House; the American people were horrified by many things they heard. In August 1974 Nixon resigned rather than face impeachment. His successor, President Gerald Ford, gave him a full pardon in September 1974.

◁ *President Nixon makes his resignation speech.*

The worst humiliation for the USA, however, came in southeast Asia, where the Vietnam War was still in progress at the start of the decade. There were massive anti-war protests in the USA, and in May 1970 four student protesters were shot dead by National Guardsmen at Kent State University, Ohio.

▷ *This photograph of one of the student protesters killed at Kent State University was taken by a fellow student who was studying journalism.*

In 1973, US troops pulled out of Vietnam after a peace agreement with communist North Vietnam. But in April 1975, North Vietnam triumphed over the USA's ally South Vietnam, and Vietnam was unified under a communist government. Communists also took power in neighbouring Cambodia and Laos.

...Newsflash...

30 April 1975. There were extraordinary scenes in Saigon, the capital of South Vietnam, yesterday as communist troops from North Vietnam entered the city. Although the last US troops left South Vietnam in 1973, thousands of American personnel were still in the city. Most were lifted out in helicopters and taken to US aircraft carriers offshore. The US embassy was besieged by panicking Vietnamese wanting a place on board the helicopters. Today, North Vietnamese tanks rolled into the centre of Saigon and the communist flag was raised over the presidential palace. The war in Vietnam is over.

△ *A South Vietnamese man tries to get on board a helicopter out of Saigon.*

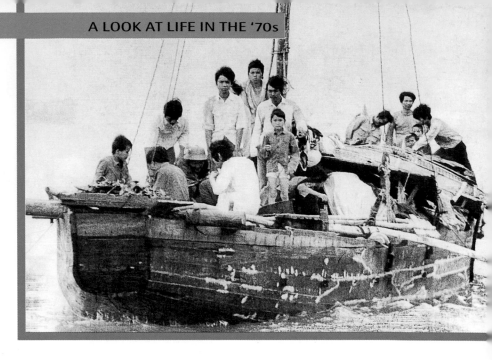

Cambodia and Vietnam

The communist triumph in Cambodia was followed by the worst horrors of the decade. The Khmer Rouge regime, led by Pol Pot, embarked on a plan to build a totally new society, which involved killing hundreds of thousands of people from the old society. Around a million people probably died in Pol Pot's notorious Killing Fields.

Vietnam was also a difficult place to live after the communist victory. Driven by economic hardship and persecution, many thousands of 'boat people' fled Vietnam by sea.

△ These Vietnamese 'boat people' had sailed 600 miles across the South China Sea to reach Hong Kong.

Profile

Pol Pot

Pol Pot was the leader of the communist Khmer Rouge, who took power in Cambodia in 1975 after a long and bitter guerrilla war. Once in power, Pol Pot tried to create a completely new society. He drove the inhabitants of the Cambodian capital, Phnom Penh, into the countryside to work in the fields. Huge numbers died of disease or ill-treatment. Many thousands more were killed because Pol Pot saw them as enemies of his regime. In 1979, Pol Pot was driven from power when Vietnam invaded Cambodia. He died in 1998.

Terrorism

Terrorism grabbed the headlines throughout the 1970s. Much of it centred around the Palestinian Arabs' hatred of Israel. Palestinian terrorist groups 'skijacked' airliners, carried out massacres at airports, and even held Olympic athletes hostage. In Europe, left-wing terrorists took politicians and businessmen as their targets. The Baader Meinhof gang terrorized West Germany, while in Italy the Red Brigades kidnapped and murdered prominent political leader Aldo Moro.

△ Head of the Baader Meinhof group, Ulrike Meinhof, aged 37, is arrested, 1972.

The terrorists in Europe were mostly young people from well-off backgrounds. Many had taken part in student protests in the 1960s. They had come to feel that violence was the only way to make a revolution that would change society for the better. Small groups in the USA, mostly either former student radicals or African Americans, also turned to guns and bombs to make a revolution.

Britain's major terrorist problem originated in Northern Ireland, which descended into a chaos of bombing and shooting as the Catholic IRA (Irish Republican Army) fought the British Army, and Protestant terrorists carried out attacks on Catholics. The IRA took their terrorist campaign to the British mainland, with outrages such as the bombing of a Birmingham pub in November 1974, which killed 17 people.

...Newsflash...

Munich, 5 September 1972. Early this morning, eight Palestinian terrorists entered the Munich Olympic village, where athletes taking part in this year's Games are housed. They broke into the building where the Israeli Olympic team was staying, killed two Israelis who tried to resist, and took nine athletes and officials hostage. German police allowed the terrorists to travel with their hostages to an airport, but there the police marksmen opened fire. In the fighting that followed, five terrorists, all nine hostages, and a policeman were killed.

▷ In 1970, Palestinian terrorists forced three hi-jacked airliners (British, Swiss and American) to fly to Dawson's Field in the Jordan desert. They blew up the planes and took the passengers and crews hostage. The hostages were eventually set free in return for the release of Palestinian prisoners.

▷ *An Egyptian soldier celebrates the successful attack across the Suez Canal that opened Egypt's 1973 war with Israel. The attack took place on the Jewish festival of Yom Kippur.*

Economy in turmoil

In 1973, Israel once more fought a major war against its Arab neighbours. The Yom Kippur War, as it was called, resulted in an oil embargo by the Middle East oil producers – they refused to sell oil to Western countries. This plunged the world economy into turmoil. Oil prices rocketed. The 'oil sheikhs' became rich and powerful, while Western governments had to struggle with inflation and mass unemployment. This was a shock to people in Europe and North America, who had become used to full employment and rapid economic growth, which had lasted for almost 30 years.

▽ *Drivers in Western countries found ways of dealing with petrol shortages in 1973. This car in Denmark was adapted to run on beech wood.*

In the second half of the 1970s, as unemployment mounted, many disillusioned youths in Britain and the USA turned to aggressive 'punk' styles and music to express their hostility to a society that had failed to live up to their expectations.

British troubles

Despite joining the European Community, along with Denmark, in 1973, Britain was especially hard hit by economic problems in the 1970s. Trade unions challenged governments in waves of large-scale strikes. In the winter of 1973-74, the Conservative government of Edward Heath introduced a three-day working week as supplies of fuel ran out because of a coalminers' strike. In 1978-79 it was a Labour government under James Callaghan that faced a wave of strikes in the 'Winter of Discontent' – rubbish piled up in the streets, and even gravediggers went on strike.

...Newsflash...

29 November 1978. More than 900 people have died in a mass suicide at Jonestown, Guyana. They were members of a religious cult, the People's Temple, led by Reverend Jim Jones. The tragedy occurred after a California Congressman, Leo Ryan, arrived in Jonestown to investigate the cult. Ryan and four people accompanying him were shot by People's Temple security guards. Jones then ordered his entire group to commit suicide by drinking cyanide-laced fruit juice. The dead include 276 children.

Progress for democracy

The political news of the 1970s was not all bad, of course. In Portugal, Spain and Greece, authoritarian governments were replaced by democracies. In the communist bloc, dissidents challenged the power of the Soviet Union. They included the author Aleksandr Solzhenitsyn, who was exiled to the West in 1974. The election of a Polish pope, John Paul II, in 1978, encouraged opposition to communist government in Poland. In China, the death of communist leader Mao Tse-tung in 1976 was followed by a greater openness to Western trade and free enterprise.

Turning away from liberation

During the 1970s, many ordinary people felt that 'liberation' had gone too far. They wanted more order and authority. A sign of the changing times was the execution of murderer Gary Gilmore in Utah in 1977. This ended a ten-year period in which no executions had taken place in the USA.

In 1979, Margaret Thatcher was elected British prime minister. In the USA, Ronald Reagan who, as governor of California, had fought student protesters, was elected president in 1980. Reagan and Thatcher were completely opposed to many of the developments of the previous 20 years. Their arrival in power brought in a new era.

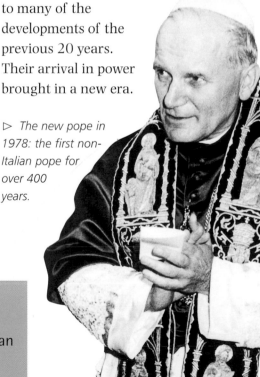

▷ *The new pope in 1978: the first non-Italian pope for over 400 years.*

In a radio programme broadcast by the BBC Russian service in 1979, Aleksandr Solzhenitsyn said:

'For us in Russia, communism is a dead dog, while, for many people in the West, it is still a living lion.'

A LOOK AT
SCIENCE and TECHNOLOGY
IN THE '70s

The 1970s was a decade when many people lost faith in technological progress, because they believed that it was destroying the natural environment. But at the same time, progress in electronics began to have a major impact on people's daily lives.

In 1971, the US company Intel produced the first silicon chips, the tiny microprocessors that would soon allow computers to become many times smaller, more powerful and cheaper than before. The first computers sold to the general public were pocket calculators, marketed from 1972. The first personal computer (PC), the Aetair 8800, went on sale in the USA in 1975.

Goodbye
Gas-guzzling cars; manned Moon landings

Hello
Video recorders; pocket calculators; Greenpeace; test-tube babies; Moog synthesizers

◁ A record of 'Sounds of the Earth' (and instructions for playing it) were prepared to be carried on Voyager 2, in case the spacecraft should meet other life on its journey through the solar system.

Urging technologists to concentrate on real needs, E. F. Schumacher wrote in 1973:

'Small is beautiful. To go for giantism is to go for self-destruction.'

Successes and failures
Not every novelty was a success. In 1971, quadraphonic sound was hailed as the next step forward from stereo. Everyone would soon have four speakers instead of two – one in each corner of the room. But quadraphonics simply never took off, perhaps because people didn't want to have to sit exactly in the middle of their room in order to listen to music.

Video recorders, on the other hand, first marketed in 1972, rapidly became a popular success. By the end of the decade they had begun to be seen as standard household items. Colour televisions also became commonplace in Europe and the USA in the course of the decade. By 1979 very few American families still watched TV in black and white.

▷ A sign of the end of the Space Race: cosmonaut Leonov (top) meets astronauts Slayton and Stafford when the Soviet Soyuz and the US Apollo craft dock in space in July 1975.

...Newsflash...

20 July 1976. The Viking 1 spacecraft landed safely on Mars today after an 11-month journey from the Earth. The unmanned craft sent back clear pictures of the Red Planet's rocky desert surface. It will dig up samples of Mars dust and analyse them, searching for signs of life. So far, however, it appears as if the Martians are nowhere to be seen.

Space exploration

The space programmes of both the USA and the Soviet Union ran into problems at the start of the 1970s. In April 1970, America's Apollo 13 manned Moon flight almost ended in disaster after an oxygen leak. The crew returned to Earth safely but hazardously in their lunar module. A year later, three Soviet cosmonauts were less lucky. They died during the journey back to Earth from the space station Salyut 1.

In December 1972, the USA sent its last manned craft to the Moon. The Space Race between the USA and the Soviet Union was over. In July 1975, a US and a Soviet spacecraft met up in space, symbolizing a new era of cooperation. Both countries sent unmanned space vehicles to explore the planets. A Soviet craft landed on Venus in 1975, and a US craft landed on Mars the following year. In 1977, the USA launched the space probes Voyager 1 and Voyager 2 on a vast journey to the end of the solar system and beyond.

◁ A picture of the surface of Mars, taken by the Viking 1 lander. NASA scientists called this large rock 'Big Joe'.

Medical progress

Scientists continued to make progress in medicine and in the understanding of the human body. Research into how babies are made led to new hope for people who wanted children but could not have them naturally. In 1978, the first 'test-tube baby', Louise Brown, was born at a hospital in the UK.

Medical advances also continued to give hope of longer life. By the end of the decade, the killer epidemic disease smallpox had been virtually eradicated through inoculation campaigns.

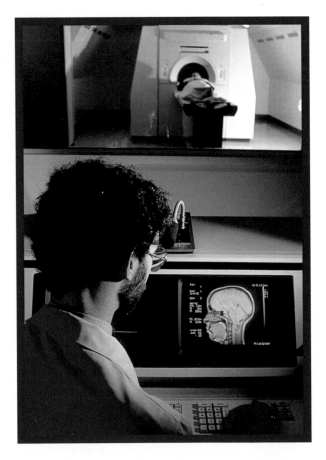

Sophisticated scanning equipment, including CAT and NMR scanners, were developed to allow doctors to see what was happening inside the body. Scientists also began to exploit genetic engineering. By 1980, this allowed Harvard scientists to produce interferon – a natural substance that fights viruses – artificially.

...Newsflash...

25 July 1978. In Oldham General and District Hospital today, a baby was born who had started life in a test-tube. Louise Brown's parents John and Lesley were unable to have children. Doctors Robert Edwards and Patrick Steptoe took an egg from Lesley and joined it with John's sperm in their laboratory. The embryo that resulted was then placed back inside Lesley's body, where it developed in the usual way. Louise is reported to be normal and healthy.

◁ *An NMR (Nuclear Magnetic Resonance) scan is made of a person's brain. Inside the detector (top), a huge magnetic field changes the arrangement of atomic particles in the body tissues. Then the magnetic field is interrupted and the particles spin back to their original arrangement. As they do so, they give off signals, which a computer can process to give the image on the screen.*

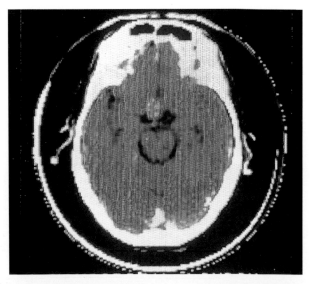

△ *One of the first CAT (Computed Axial Tomography) scans of the brain (the blue and brown areas).*

▷ In July 1976, a cloud of poisonous gas was released from a chemicals factory near the village of Seveso in northern Italy. Animals in the area began to die in large numbers and the human population was rapidly evacuated.

The ecology movement

By the start of the 1970s, ecology had become a buzz word. The public had realized that pollution was a serious threat to life systems on Earth. For the first time, people were becoming aware that handy products such as detergents and plastics had a cost in terms of the damage they caused to the environment.

In April 1970, millions of Americans took part in the first Earth Day, organized by conservationists to increase public awareness of environmental issues. In 1971, Greenpeace was founded as an international organization to struggle against damage to the environment. The following year the United Nations (UN) organized the Stockholm Conference on the Human Environment, the first major international summit on the ecology issue.

Lists of endangered species were drawn up and measures taken to stop hunting or trade in these animals. A major international campaign began to 'Save the Whales'. In 1972, the UN called for a ten-year ban on whaling, although many countries were slow to respond.

The idea that economic growth was necessarily a good thing was challenged by a group of economic experts called the Club of Rome. In a report called *The Limits to Growth* they claimed that if economies went on expanding, natural resources would be exhausted and the environment destroyed.

In 1974, scientists first warned that chlorofluorocarbons (CFCs), used in fridges and

In a book of 1971, 'The Closing Circle', Barry Commoner warned of ecological disaster in the near future, writing:

'The evidence is overwhelming that the way in which we now live on Earth is driving its thin, life-supporting skin, and ourselves with it, to destruction.'

in aerosol cans, were damaging the ozone layer, which protects us against harmful radiation from the sun. In 1978, Sweden became the first country to ban aerosols.

During the 1970s, ecological concerns affected transport. There was more emphasis on fuel economy in the design of cars, as well as on safety. The Anglo-French supersonic airliner Concorde came into service, but it met with resistance in the USA because of its environmental impact – it was too noisy and too polluting.

◁ An oil production platform in the North Sea. The 'flare boom' on the right burns off excess gas from the oil well.

expensive and supplies were thought to be running out, so all through the 1970s there was a search for alternative sources of energy. While ecologists favoured wind or wave power, most governments favoured nuclear power. But people increasingly questioned how safe this was. In March 1979, a major accident occurred at the Three Mile Island nuclear power station in Pennsylvania, USA. Although no one was killed, the accident severely undermined confidence in the future of nuclear energy.

Alternative energy

The first crude oil was pumped ashore from platforms in the North Sea in 1975. But oil was

Profile

Karen Silkwood

Karen Silkwood worked at a plant producing plutonium fuels for nuclear power stations. The plant, in Oklahoma, was owned by Kerr-McGee Nuclear Corporation. Silkwood became convinced that she and other workers at the plant were being exposed to dangerous radiation and that plutonium was going missing. On 13 November 1974 she was killed in a car crash while on her way to tell what she knew to a reporter. Many people consider the circumstances of her death suspicious. She was only 28 years old.

A LOOK AT
FASHION
IN THE '70s

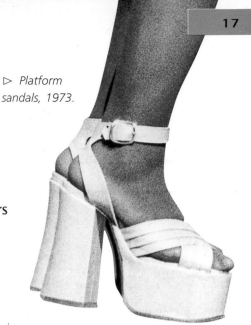

▷ *Platform sandals, 1973.*

The first half of the 1970s continued the Hippie-inspired styles and ideas of the late 1960s. There were no rules and no limits. Freedom was the buzz word. Fashion designers abandoned the old rules of good taste, producing more and more outrageous clothes. For the first time, people took to heart the idea that they could wear what they liked where and when they wanted. Generally, they wanted informality.

The years of excess and bad taste

Early 1970s style was like a fancy-dress parade. There were outrageous flares known as bell-bottoms, huge platform shoes, wide lapels and broad 'kipper' ties. Bright and clashing colours were worn by everyone. Men often sported polyester shirts with ruffles, combined with ultra suede jacket and trousers. Women were often seen in lycra bodystockings or wearing dresses slit to the top of the thigh. Glam rock stars, such as David Bowie, Freddie Mercury and Gary Glitter, popularized the wearing of dramatic skin-tight clothing in lycra and lurex together with hefty platform shoes or boots. They also wore make-up.

The Hippie look went mainstream. Long hair for men became almost universal among the young. Rebels were forced to wear very long hair indeed to make themselves stand out.

▷ *Early 1970s fashion, as worn by the Bee Gees.*

In bad taste

Flares;
jeans;
ethnic look;
wide lapels;
platform shoes;
leather;
body piercing;
permed hair;
anything goes

Celebrating the fact that people in the 1970s were free to choose their own style, 'Vogue' magazine told its readers:

'The real star of the fashion picture is the wearer ... you.'

For men, beards, moustaches and sideburns were in. Young women and some men permed their long hair into masses of curls, to create the 'shaggy' look.

▷ *Bellbottom trousers and jeans, flaring out from the knees but tight at the hips, were a popular '70s fashion item.*

◁ *These hot pants, knee-length socks and embroidered jacket were modelled in 1971.*

An ethnic look flourished in ponchos, Afghan coats and romantic ankle-length floral or patchwork dresses. Tie-dye shirts and scarves were also popular. Everyone was wearing jeans, usually tight-fitting around the hips with enormous flares at the bottom. Some jeans were decorated with embroidery or studs, and some had floral material sewn into the flares.

Skimpy 'hot pants' enjoyed a brief period of popularity with young women early in the decade. Made of luxurious fabrics, such as velvet or silk, hot pants were extremely short shorts, and were often teamed with suede knee-high boots or maxi coats.

Some young people had been wearing maxi-length coats and dresses since 1968, but it was not until 1970 that fashion

Profile

Yves Saint Laurent

Regarded as one of the foremost designers of the 1960s and 1970s, French designer Yves Saint Laurent opened his own haute couture house in 1962.

In 1971 he declared that he was going to concentrate on ready-to-wear for young working women. He gave a rather masculine quality to his women's daywear, responding to the influence of Women's Lib. But for evening wear he kept to romantic and seductive Hippie-influenced designs.

designers, such as Yves Saint Laurent, featured midi- and maxi-length garments in their collections. The mini-skirt had become extremely popular by then, and it took another two years before women generally adopted the longer-looking styles. Even then, the mini did not disappear. Many women chose to wear maxi-length coats with mini-skirts underneath.

▷ *Fashionable colours of the decade were brown, orange and olive green.*

In an article entitled 'The Great Hemline Hassle', 'Life' magazine said in 1970:

'The latest word is long but ... many women and all men hate to see the Mini go.'

Profile

Vivienne Westwood

Outrageous British designer Vivienne Westwood was prominent throughout the '70s and '80s. She opened her own shop in the King's Road in London in 1971. By the mid-1970s, influenced by the street style of rebellious city youth, she was taking many of the more extreme elements of the punk look into her designs. Her punk collection included ripped T-shirts, necklines dipping under one arm and T-shirts printed with swastikas and pornographic images. Westwood achieved international recognition in 1981 with her 'new romantic' collection, which evolved out of punk.

'Radical chic'

'Cool' young African American men adopted a flashy style associated with hip street-funk music. They combined ruffled silk shirts or close-fitting black turtleneck sweaters with fantastically flared trousers – not jeans – always extremely tight-fitting around the hips. To complete the look, they wore leather or vinyl midi- or maxi-length coats, platform shoes with at least 12-cm heels and sometimes a black hat with turn-down brim. Singer James Brown did much to popularize the style, as did the 1971 'blaxploitation' film *Shaft*.

At the same time, traditional African clothes, such as the 'dashiki', and clothes featuring African patterns continued to be popular with many as part of the ethnic look. And many African Americans emphasized their origins by wearing huge Afro hairstyles.

▽ *Newcomer Richard Rowntree starred in 'Shaft'.*

▷ *Inger, a Swedish punk rock fan, with a safety pin through her cheek and a swastika tattoo on her face, 1977.*

Punk styles

The mood of fashion changed completely in the second half of the 1970s. The 'peace and love' pose of the Hippies was replaced by an aggressive 'me first' attitude. Along with the extreme 'punk' look came a more conservative 'dress for success' look which owed much to the styles of the early 1960s.

Many punks pierced their bodies, too, wearing safety pins in their cheeks, ears and lips. They deliberately used trashy materials, such as plastic, in vulgar colours. Some even wore black rubbish sacks. A young person with an appearance like this was not just unemployed but unemployable. British fashion designer Vivienne Westwood included elements of punk style in the clothes she sold.

The punk movement of the mid-1970s was aggressively anti-establishment and anti-Hippie. With the violent music of such bands as the Sex Pistols and Siouxsie and the Banshees went hairstyles and clothing that horrified most people. Punk fashion was worn in its extreme only by a few young people, and mostly in Britain. Punk youths spiked their hair or shaved the sides of their heads to create Mohican haircuts, which they then bleached or dyed black or pink. They wore heavy black make-up over whitened faces. Ripped T-shirts and Doc Marten boots were essential, and sometimes worn with torn fishnet stockings. Punks decorated their T-shirts, black leather jackets and army surplus trousers with swastikas, studs, chains and safety pins.

Dressing for success

In the late 1970s, fans of New Wave and Mod Revival bands also rejected Hippie long hair and casualness, but in favour of a sharper look. As in the pre-Flower Power early 1960s, young men cut their hair short and had narrow bottoms to their trousers.

At the same time, mainstream fashion designers, such as Italian designer Giorgio Armani, began producing more classic designs billed as 'real clothes for real people'. They featured skirts that finished just below the knee, straight-cut trousers for men and women and 'dress for success' suits. During the decade, women increasingly chose to wear trousers, especially in the male-dominated workplace, where they were anxious to be taken seriously.

A LOOK AT
POP MUSIC
IN THE '70s

Like 1970s clothes, 1970s music showed a varied mix of colourful styles. There was an abundance of talent, from David Bowie to Bruce Springsteen and from Abba to Blondie. Former Beatles Paul McCartney and John Lennon pursued successful solo careers, and Bob Marley made reggae one of the biggest musical trends of the decade. It was the decade of the supergroup and the stadium band, and punk and New Wave. It was also the decade of the teenybopper and disco fever.

Glam rock and slick pop
Early in the decade some performers, such as Elton John, attracted attention by dressing in an eccentrically flamboyant way. Others, such as David Bowie, Marc Bolan, Gary Glitter, Freddy

△ In the early 1970s, British singer David Bowie linked his music to a flamboyant stage performance.

Mercury and Kiss, went a step further by wearing dramatic make-up as well. They created a new category of rock called 'glam rock'.

Profile

Bob Marley

From the Trench Town ghetto of Kingstown, Jamaica, charismatic reggae singer-songwriter Bob Marley, and his band, the Wailers, achieved international recognition with the release of their third album, *Bob Marley and the Wailers Live,* in 1975. Hailed as 'the black Bob Dylan', Marley was passionately committed to the cause of the poor and the oppressed. He brought reggae music into the mainstream with such classic songs as 'No Woman No Cry', 'Natty Dread' and 'War'. Tragically, his career was cut short on 11 May 1981 when he died of cancer.

...Newsflash...

New York, 1 August 1971. More than 40,000 young people flocked to Madison Square Garden tonight, to the first major charity rock show. Organized by former Beatle George Harrison, the concert should raise more than $250,000 for the two million refugees of Bangladesh, where civil war has led to epidemics of cholera and smallpox. A recent convert to Eastern wisdom, Harrison now names Indian sitarist Ravi Shankar among his close friends. Shankar opened the show. Other performers included Eric Clapton, Leon Russell, Ringo Starr, George Harrison and Bob Dylan.

▽ *In 1975, tickets for all ten gigs played by New Jersey singer-songwriter Bruce Springsteen were sold out in advance. Posters advertizing the gigs and Springsteen's new album, 'Born to Run', bore the words: 'I have seen the future of rock'n'roll and its name is Bruce Springsteen.'*

▽ *The Swedish group Abba consisted of two married couples, Anni-Frid Lyngstad and Benny Andersson, and Bjorn Ulvaeus and Agnetha Faltskog.*

The enormously successful Swedish pop group Abba provided a toned-down version of glam rock. Eurovision song contest winners with their song 'Waterloo' in 1974, Abba achieved 19 worldwide hits during the decade with their slick brand of pop. Their world sales totalled 150 million, matching those of the Beatles.

Teenybopper appeal

Pop fans were getting younger, and many bands of the early 1970s had predominantly teen-appeal. After featuring in the TV series, *The Partridge Family*, in 1970, David Cassidy became the leading teen idol of this period with hits such as 'How can I be Sure?' and 'Daydreamer'.

Les McKeown, singer with the teenybopper band the Bay City Rollers, remarked in 1977:

'Psychologically it can be a real drag, all the travelling, never getting out of the hotel. But I think it'll mature eventually and they'll just scream at the end of numbers instead of all the way through.'

△ *Left to right: Jay, Wayne, Merrill, Donny and Alan Osmond, with eight-year-old Jimmy Osmond in the centre, May 1972.*

The Osmond family were major teen favourites. In 1972 Donny Osmond had a chart-topping hit with 'Puppy Love', his sister Marie had a huge hit with 'Paper Roses', and youngest brother 'Little' Jimmy joined in with 'Long Haired Lover from Liverpool'.

The Osmonds were as young as their audiences, and the same was true of key members of the Jackson Five, whose pulsating dance music was a favourite with teenyboppers. The group's lead singer, Michael Jackson, was only 12 at the start of the decade.

◁ *The Jackson Five rose to fame as a teenybopper band in 1970. The youngest of the five brothers, Michael Jackson (centre), later became a superstar in his own right.*

Disco craze

Disco dance music became a major trend in the wake of the huge success of the movie *Saturday Night Fever* in 1977, starring John Travolta. The Bee Gees were the main contributors to the movie soundtrack, and they topped the charts on both sides of the Atlantic with all six of the songs they had performed in the film. *Saturday Night Fever* turned out to be the biggest-selling soundtrack album of all time, with more than one million copies sold.

One of the classiest and most successful dance bands of the disco boom was Chic, who scored a string of dance hits during 1978 and 1979, including 'Everybody Dance' and 'Le Freak'. During the same two years, camp disco group Village People – who performed dressed as a biker, a construction worker, an Indian chief, a cowboy, a policeman and a GI – had enormous international hits with 'YMCA', 'In the Navy' and 'Go West'.

...Newsflash...

New York, December 1977. The latest cult for young movie-goers is this year's surprise hit, *Saturday Night Fever*. The movie stars little-known actor and dancer John Travolta as Tony Manero, king of the Brooklyn disco scene. The dance numbers by the Bee Gees have audiences bopping in the aisles and the spin-off album looks set to be one of the most successful soundtrack releases ever. The movie reflects the growing craze for disco dancing, which is generating its own brand of up-beat pop music, a world away from the aggression and social comment of punk.

△ *In The Who's rock opera, 'Tommy', Roger Daltrey played a 'deaf, dumb and blind kid' who was the 'pinball wizard'.*

Serious rock music

By the start of the '70s, many rock musicians had begun to take themselves very seriously. The Who performed their rock opera *Tommy* – based on a double album released in 1968 – at New York's Metropolitan Opera House in 1970. In 1975 a movie adaptation of *Tommy* was released, made by British director Ken Russell.

The same year Queen achieved million-seller success with the symphonic rock single 'Bohemian Rhapsody'. A long way from the simple singles of the early Beatles era, this six-minute-long track was accompanied by one of the first pop videos.

'Progressive' rock was popular among students and pop listeners in their 20s – people who had been teenagers in the late 1960s. Groups such as Yes, Pink Floyd, Genesis and the Electric Light Orchestra (ELO) took advantage of the huge improvements being made to the sound and range of electric instruments and the range of facilities offered by recording studios.

album *Tales from Topographic Oceans*, featuring a powerful mix of sounds and lengthy song cycles, was a huge success in 1974. A year earlier, Mike Oldfield's *Tubular Bells*, using a wide range of classical and rock instruments, achieved overwhelming international success. Another band that made 'rock symphonies' was ELO.

◁ *Vocalist and flautist Ian Anderson led the subversive Hippie band Jethro Tull.*

Some progressive rock bands created extraordinary stage performances, using the latest laser technology and vast theatrical sets. In their 1977 US tour, Pink Floyd's stage act featured an enormous inflatable pig, symbol of their latest album, *Animals*. In 1978, ELO's act included a life-size spacecraft.

People's home playing equipment had also improved, allowing them to appreciate the more sophisticated rock sounds being produced.

Rock groups disappeared for months at a time to record concept albums. Pink Floyd's highly successful *Dark Side of the Moon* belonged to this category. So, too, did *Desperado* and *Hotel California*, albums produced in the mid-1970s by the West Coast rock band The Eagles. Rick Wakeman of Yes was a classically trained musician, and this group did most to develop the new symphonic sound. They utilized the new Moog synthesizer to enormous effect, and their

Malcolm McLaren, the Sex Pistols' manager:

'Rock is fundamentally a young people's music, right? And a lot of kids feel cheated. They feel that the music's been taken away from them by that whole over-25 audience.'

Punk and the New Wave

Punk emerged in the mid-'70s as a reaction against the overblown sounds and pompous attitudes of these rock 'dinosaurs'. Punks harked back to a time when all you needed to form a pop band was a few electric guitars and a simple amplifier. They wanted rock to be crude and aggressive again, without pretending to be 'art'. In Britain, rebellious teenagers flocked to see subversive punk performers Iggy Pop, the Sex Pistols, the Clash, the Damned, the Buzzcocks and the Stranglers. Banned by the BBC, the Sex Pistols' 'God Save the Queen' reached number 2 in the UK singles charts in 1977. In New York from 1975 a thriving club scene featured the raw energy of the Ramones, Patti Smith, Blondie and Talking Heads. Their music had the aggression and rebellious values of the British punk scene but

△ US punk group, the Ramones.

without the wild anarchy and extremism – the US bands could really play their instruments.

As punk became calmer and more sophisticated towards the end of the decade, the result was dubbed 'New Wave'. Key New Wave performers in Britain included the Jam, the Pretenders, Elvis Costello, the Boomtown Rats and the Police.

Profile

Sid Vicious

The violent, sneering bass player of punk band the Sex Pistols, Sid Vicious was hired by manager Macolm McLaren in 1977, to replace the musically able Glen Matlock. Vicious famously could not play his instrument at all, but had plenty of ugly aggression. Responsible for many outbreaks of violence at press conferences and gigs, Vicious was charged with the murder of his girlfriend, Nancy Spungen, on 13 October 1978. Released on bail, he died from a heroin overdose on 2 February 1979. He was 21 years old.

A LOOK AT
ART and ARCHITECTURE
IN THE '70s

There was enormous public interest in art and culture in the 1970s. The numbers of people visiting art galleries and museums rose dramatically. But the works made by living artists were often a puzzle to the general public.

Much of the interest in high culture was focused on the past. The biggest museum event of the decade was the Tutankhamun exhibition, showing most of the objects found in the tomb of a young Egyptian pharaoh who died over 3,000 years ago. Queues formed outside this exhibition both in London and New York. Tutankhamun's treasures were seen by almost 2 million people in Britain, and over 8 million in the USA.

It was a time when the prices paid for works of art at auction rose astronomically. By the end of the decade paintings by artists such as Velázquez and Van Gogh were selling at auction for around $5 million (over £2 million).

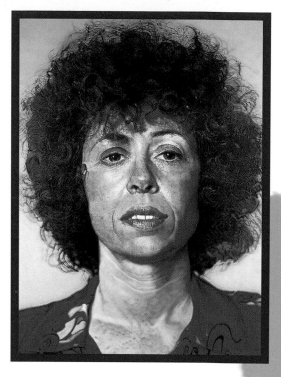

△ US artist Chuck Close became known for huge portraits, like this one of 'Linda' (1975-76), painted in a photorealist style.

Profile

Robert Smithson

American artist Robert Smithson was a leading member of the 'Earth Art' movement at the start of the 1970s. He created 'earthworks' – large sculptures in the landscape, using natural materials. His most famous earthwork, *Spiral Jetty*, was created in 1970. It is a huge spiral of earth, rock and salt crystals coiling out from the shore into Utah's Great Salt Lake. The work has a mysterious power, reminiscent of ancient monuments such as Stonehenge. Smithson died in an aircrash in 1973, while surveying a site for another earthwork in Texas.

Art not for sale

Many living artists were appalled at works of art being goods that were bought and sold. Some of them practised forms of 'conceptual art', which did not produce an art object you could sell. The most spectacular of these strange works were by the Bulgarian-born artist Christo.

In 1972 he draped 18,580 square metres of orange nylon fabric across a valley in Rifle, Colorado, to make the *Valley Curtain*. He carried out an even more spectacular project in California, where his white nylon *Running Fence* was strung out over 40 km of countryside down to the Pacific shore. *Running Fence* was taken down two weeks after it was put up, leaving no trace behind.

Photos and albums

The style known as 'photorealism' was another major trend of the 1970s. Artists painted large pictures that looked exactly like blown-up photos, with every minute detail clear and precise. Photography itself was treated with increasing respect in the 1970s, being seen as an art-form in its own right.

Record album covers also became a form of art. Perhaps the most famous were the bizarre images created for Yes albums by the British illustrator Roger Dean. The band Pink Floyd were also noted for their surreal, imaginative cover designs. Many illustrators used airbrushing – a fine spray of paint squirted from a nozzle – to create hard-edged, glossy images.

...Newsflash...

February 1976. A storm of controversy has blown up about the latest work of contemporary art to go on show at London's Tate Gallery. *Equivalent VIII* is by American artist Carl Andre. It consists of 120 ordinary housebricks laid out in a rectangle on the floor. The Tate has refused to say how much it paid for the work, but critics are saying that no money at all should have been spent on such an object.

▷ *The Bulgarian artist Christo wraps the Aurelian Wall in Rome in plastic sheeting, 1974.*

△ The Sydney Opera House. With its bizarre but beautiful shape, like sails or wings, it immediately became one of the world's most famous landmarks.

▷ Built in 1970-74, the Sears Tower in Chicago has 110 storeys and is 443 metres tall.

Exciting architecture

For the first time since the 1930s, there was a rush to build the tallest skyscraper. The World Trade Centre in New York briefly held the title in 1973, before Chicago's Sears Tower overtook it the following year.

As high culture boomed, fine new buildings were built to cater for the demand. One of these was the Sydney Opera House, designed by Danish architect Jørn Utzon. It was completed in 1973 at a cost of over $100 million.

Another success was the Pompidou Centre – an arts centre named after Georges Pompidou, president of France in 1967-74. Designed by Italian architect Renzo Piano and British architect Richard Rogers, the Pompidou Centre had a completely original look created by putting the service systems (plumbing, air conditioning ducts, etc) on the outside. Containing an art gallery, a library and much else, it was above all a fun place to be and attracted astonishing numbers of visitors.

City improvements

The building of the Pompidou Centre – or Beaubourg, as it is often called – was part of a scheme to redevelop the heart of Paris. Similar redevelopment was carried out in hundreds of places worldwide in the 1970s. The pedestrianization of city streets, begun experimentally in the late 1960s, became almost universal in historic centres. Cars were kept out and old buildings were restored and conserved, rather than being knocked down to make way for high-rise office blocks.

Indeed, it was high-rise buildings that began to be knocked down, like the Pruitt Igoe public housing blocks in St Louis, Missouri, demolished in 1972. The word postmodernism began to be used to describe a new form of architecture. The box-like, high-rise, undecorated buildings of the 1960s began to give way to a variety of buildings in different styles, some traditional, others wildly strange.

▽ *A run-down area of Paris, the 'Plateau Beaubourg', was the site chosen for building the High Tech Pompidou Centre. Most people call the centre 'Beaubourg'.*

A LOOK AT
SPORT
IN THE '70s

In the 1970s, sport was increasingly dominated by television, because TV channels were prepared to pay large amounts of money for the right to cover events. Top sports personalities earned more than ever before, a few becoming multi-millionaires.

Some sports became more important because they suited television. This was true of snooker in Britain, and of American football – with its top star O. J. Simpson of the Buffalo Bills. The old-fashioned world of cricket was torn apart in 1977 when an Australian TV boss, Kerry Packer, offered players large sums of money to desert the traditional game. No sport, it seemed, could resist the power of TV money.

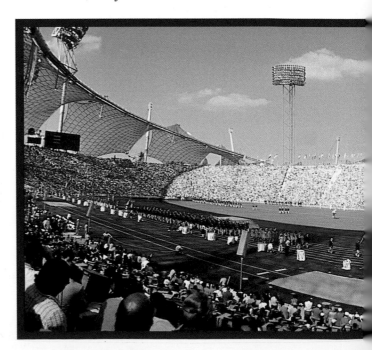

▷ *In 1972, the Munich Olympics were televised to audiences around the world. The TV journalists found themselves covering not only sports events, but also the actions of Palestinian terrorists, who broke into the Olympic Village where the Israeli team was staying. The terrorist outrage resulted in the deaths of 11 Israelis, a German policeman and five of the terrorists.*

Olympic triumphs

The Olympic Games, held in Munich in 1972 and in Montreal in 1976, produced some memorable performances. At the Munich Games, 22-year-old American swimmer Mark

Abu Daoud, one of the terrorists at the Munich Olympics, said:

'We were aware right from the beginning of the great influence of television. Our aim was to make the international community aware of the Palestinian cause.'

▷ *The opening ceremony of the Munich Olympic Games, August 1972.*

Profile

Nadia Comaneci

The outstanding star of the Montreal Olympics was the tiny Romanian gymnast Nadia Comaneci. Only 14 years old and barely 1.5 metres tall, she captured the hearts of the public with her grace and skill. She won three gold medals and a bronze in individual events, plus a silver medal in the team event. Especially memorable was the moment when the judges awarded her the first ever perfect 10 score in the history of the Olympics. Comaneci went on to win two more gold medals in the 1980 Games.

Spitz won a record seven gold medals – four for individual events and three for team relays. Gymnastics became one of the most popular Olympic events at this time. Soviet gymnast Olga Korbut enchanted the public at Munich, and at the Montreal Olympics the outstanding personality of the whole games was 14-year-old Romanian gymnast Nadia Comaneci.

Politics and the Games

But in many ways, the Olympics in the 1970s were marred by political conflicts. The terrorist outrage at the Munich Olympics was the most obvious example. More subtly, the spirit of the Games was harmed by the Cold War confrontation between the USA and the Soviet Union. The Olympics became desperate trials of strength between the Americans on one side and the Soviets and their East German allies on the other. The extraordinary performances of East German athletes and swimmers were, we now know, at least partly based on the use of banned drugs.

South Africa was permanently banned from the Games because of its white racism, but 22 black African countries still boycotted the Montreal Olympics in an anti-South Africa protest. The black Africans withdrew their teams because New Zealand was allowed to take part in the Games, even though a New Zealand rugby team had toured South Africa.

▷ *Brazilian football fans surround their hero, Pele, after Brazil's 4-1 victory in the 1970 World Cup Final.*

Galaxies of stars

The 1970s was a great time for tennis, with Chris Evert, Billie Jean King, Yvonne Goolagong and Virginia Wade competing in the women's game, and the men's game dominated by Ilie Nastase, Bjorn Borg, Jimmy Connors and Arthur Ashe. Borg won five Wimbledon singles titles in a row from 1976 to 1980.

In golf, Britain's Tony Jacklin and Spain's Seve Ballesteros had successes, but the world's best players, including Lee Trevino, Jack Nicklaus and Tom Watson, were all American.

Total football

Soccer started on a high in the 1970s. The Brazilian team that won the 1970 World Cup was possibly the greatest ever seen. Based around the skills of Pele, the world's most famous footballer, Brazil beat Italy in the final, 4-1. Holland, led by Johann Cruyff, were the other great team of the 1970s, but they never won the World Cup.

Profile

Arthur Ashe

Born in 1943 in Richmond, Virginia, Arthur Ashe was the first African American man to become a top tennis star. He was chosen to represent his country in the Davis Cup in 1963, aged 19. He won his first Grand Slam tournament, the US Open in 1968. In 1975, he took the Wimbledon singles title, beating Jimmy Connors in the final. Alongside his tennis career, Ashe was a prominent campaigner against racism. Tragically, he was infected with HIV, the AIDS virus, through a blood transfusion in the 1980s. He died in 1993.

The decade saw a determined effort to make soccer work as a professional sport in the USA. Many foreign stars were signed by the new American teams, including Pele, who signed up for New York Cosmos in 1975. The professional league was eventually a failure, as Americans continued to prefer baseball and their own brand of football. But it encouraged American kids to play soccer, which was soon to become an increasingly popular school sport.

Ali's comeback

Boxing was dominated by the extraordinary saga of American heavyweight Muhammad Ali. Formerly known as Cassius Clay, Ali had been world champion until 1967. Then he had been stripped of his title because he refused to serve as a soldier in the Vietnam War. He was allowed to return to boxing in 1970, and won the world championship title again in October 1974, when he knocked out George Foreman in a fight held in Zaire, central Africa.

To everyone's surprise, Ali went on boxing for another five years. He lost the world championship to Leon Spinks in February 1978, but won it back later in the year. He is the only boxer to have won the title three times.

▽ In 1974 US baseball player Hank Aaron surpassed Babe Ruth's 39-year-old record of career home runs. Aaron retired in 1976, after 22 years in the sport, with a total of 755 home runs.

...Newsflash...

29 October 1974. In a classic fight that has been dubbed 'the rumble in the jungle', 32-year-old Muhammad Ali defeated 25-year-old George Foreman to regain the world heavyweight championship he lost in 1967. The contest was held in the sweltering heat of Kinshasa, the capital of the central African state of Zaire. Ali knocked out his opponent in the eighth round of the fight to confirm that he is still 'the greatest'.

A LOOK AT
LEISURE and ENTERTAINMENT
IN THE '70s

By the end of the 1970s, American magazines were calling it the 'Me Decade'. In the course of the decade many people turned away from trying to change the world to concentrate instead on changing themselves. In general, people became more concerned with improving their health, their looks, and the way they felt about the world.

Jogging grew from an activity practised by a small minority of people into a craze for health-conscious Americans. Aerobics also took off as a trendy form of exercise. Smoking and drinking alcohol were increasingly frowned upon – although more women smoked and drank than ever before.

▷ *From the early 1970s, going to an aerobic dance class became a fashionable way of keeping fit.*

Health foods became popular, as part of a swing towards 'natural' products. There was also a boom in diet drinks and slimming foods, such as fat-free yoghurt.

66 99

Veteran Indian jogger Jinabhai Navik expressed the new fitness philosophy of the 1970s:

'If you want to live, you must walk. If you want to live long, you must run.'

Exotic therapies, including crystal healing and acupuncture, won many followers. Increasing numbers of people turned to yoga or meditation to improve their spiritual health as well as their physical condition.

There was a boom in 'self-help' books on how to 'know yourself' and develop your talents and creativity. Self-expression and self-liberation were widely pursued goals. Increasingly, people were prepared to 'let it all hang out'.

Streaking – throwing your clothes off and running naked across sports grounds or in other public places – was

▽ *Britons turned out in millions to celebrate the Queen's Silver Jubilee – the 25th anniversary of her coronation.*

...Newsflash...

4 July 1976. The USA is 200 years old today, and Americans have been celebrating from coast to coast, showing they can enjoy themselves in peace and harmony – and with a sense of fun. Hundreds of thousands of New Yorkers watched as a fleet of sailing ships progressed up the Hudson River. In Washington, laser beams wrote 'Happy Birthday, USA' in the sky. In Boston, they celebrated 1776 by making a pancake 193 cm across, and in Wisconsin enthusiasts spun 1,776 frisbees into the sky.

invented in the 1970s and quickly developed into a craze. Topless sunbathing for women became commonplace on beaches in many European countries, although it was not found acceptable in the USA.

Goodbye
Black and white TVs and movies;
Elvis Presley;
John Wayne;
Charlie Chaplin

Hello
Smilie faces;
jogging;
McDonalds;
streakers;
music cassettes;
computer games;
the Muppets;
Rubik's cube

In the USA, especially, there was a strong trend for people to be nicer to one another. Americans put 'smilie face' stickers on their cars and clothes and said 'have a nice day' a lot more in restaurants and shops. The Bicentennial festivities in 1976 – celebrating the 200th anniversary of American independence – were a happy time for many in the USA. In 1977, Britons celebrated the 25th anniversary of Queen Elizabeth II's coronation.

▷ *Hungarian design professor Erno Rubik built geometric models as a hobby. His 'Rubik's Cube' puzzle began to be sold in 1977 and was marketed worldwide by 1980. Players twisted the 26 small cubes out of their original arrangement and then tried to put them back to the way they were.*

Profile

Jodie Foster

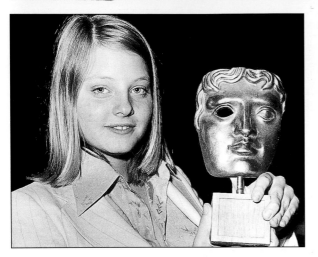

△ Jodie Foster won this Best Supporting Actress Award for her performance in the movie 'Bugsie Malone'.

Born in 1962, Jodie Foster was a successful child actor in the early 1970s, appearing in Disney movies such as *Tom Sawyer*. Many people were shocked when, at the age of 13, she played the part of a drug-addicted teenage prostitute in the violent movie *Taxi Driver*. Although controversial, this performance made her a worldwide reputation. She continued her education alongside her acting career, graduating from Yale University with a degree in literature. Since growing up, she has twice won Oscars for best actress, in *The Accused* (1988) and *The Silence of the Lambs* (1991).

At the movies

People did not go to the movies as much as before, partly because ticket prices had gone up sharply. But audiences would pack cinemas for a few hit movies each year. As a result, the 1970s was a decade dominated by a small number of 'blockbusters' that pulled in the crowds and made lots of money. These movies were so important to Hollywood that the studios began making sequels, to cash in on the success of the original.

In the first half of the 1970s, many movies were made that exploited the new freedoms won in the previous decade. They showed more extreme violence or more explicit sex than had ever been allowed before. *Last Tango in Paris*, starring Marlon Brando, and director Stanley Kubrick's *Clockwork Orange* were movies that shocked audiences at the time.

Many hit movies in the early 1970s were gloomy heavyweight productions, such as *The Godfather*, made by Francis Ford Coppola, and

▽ Sylvester Stallone (centre) was an unknown bit-part actor until he wrote and starred in the Oscar-winning movie 'Rocky' in 1976.

◁ *Steven Spielberg's 'Close Encounters of the Third Kind' (1977) was a story of contact between humans and extraterrestrials.*

Super stars

Actors discovered in the 1970s included Robert De Niro and Al Pacino, both of whom appeared in the *Godfather* series. Ryan O'Neal and Ali McGraw were new stars in the 1970 weepy *Love Story*. Sylvester Stallone emerged as macho hero Rocky, and Christopher Reeve was a massive hit as Superman. Other already well-known stars earned new respect. Clint Eastwood went from strength to strength, with movies such as *Dirty Harry* and *The Outlaw Josie Wales*. Woody Allen developed from a zany comic into a respected filmmaker with the 1978 Oscar-winner *Annie Hall*. And Jane Fonda won admiration for her acting talent in films such as *Klute* and *The China Syndrome*.

Martin Scorsese's *Mean Streets* and *Taxi Driver*. Later in the decade, movies lightened up. There was a swing back to making entertainment movies for a family audience. New filmmaker Steven Spielberg had huge hits with *Jaws* and the science-fiction blockbuster *Close Encounters of the Third Kind*. Director George Lucas made the first of the *Star Wars* series in 1977.

Robert Redford

Blond, blue-eyed Robert Redford appeared in many of the top movies of the 1970s. He teamed up with Paul Newman in the 1973 blockbuster *The Sting*, an Oscar-winning movie about two confidence tricksters. In 1976 he starred with Dustin Hoffman in the thriller *All the President's Men*, about the two *Washington Post* journalists whose investigations triggered the Watergate scandal. Other Redford hits included the cynical political movie *The Candidate* in 1972 and *The Way We Were*, 1973.

▷ *Redford in 'All the President's Men'.*

Something for everyone

Overall, there was something for everyone in 1970s cinema. Horror movies were more horrible than ever – big hits included *The Exorcist*, *Halloween* and *Alien*. Disaster movies also did well, with major box-office successes including *Airport* in 1970 and *The Towering Inferno* in 1974. Chinese American actor Bruce Lee made kung-fu movies a cult with a wide following. And 'blaxploitation' films such as *Shaft* – raunchy action movies aimed at a black American audience – were one of the decade's most successful innovations.

An alternative to movies for an evening out, at least in the big cities, was the new breed of rock musicals. The most successful of these, *Jesus Christ Superstar* and *Evita*, made the

◁ *John Cleese was one member of the Monty Python team, who introduced a new, absurd style of comedy in their TV show 'Monty Python's Flying Circus' and movies such as 'And Now For Something Completely Different', made in 1972. Later in the 1970s, Cleese starred in another ground-breaking TV comedy series, 'Fawlty Towers'.*

lyric writer Tim Rice and composer Andrew Lloyd Webber household names.

Staying in

Television switched from black and white to colour in the 1970s, and there were plenty of bright, lively programmes to take advantage of the new glossy look. Probably the most successful of all was *Dallas*, the CBS prime-time glamour soap about the Ewing family in oil-rich Texas. *M*A*S*H*, a long-running comedy

Profile

Alex Haley

Alex Haley grew up in Henning, Tennessee. Older members of his African American family often told stories of their ancestor Kunta Kinte, who had been brought over from Africa as a slave. These accounts later inspired Haley to write *Roots: The Saga of an American Family*, published in 1976. An historical novel, blending fact and fiction, it was the basis for the most successful television mini-series of the 1970s. Its last episode, in February 1977, was viewed by 80 million people in the USA.

...Newsflash...

29 May 1977. An 11-year-old English boy, Nigel Short, has become the youngest person ever to qualify for a national chess championship. His success pinpoints the rising interest in the game among young people in Europe and in the USA. This partly dates from 1972, when American Bobby Fischer beat the Russian master Boris Spassky in an exciting chess world championship series in Iceland.

series set in a Korean War military hospital, was also a huge popular hit. Its cynical attitude to the war appealed to a public disillusioned with US involvement in Vietnam.

The influence of the Women's Movement made itself felt on television. Female stars still had to be glamorous, but they began to be shown in leading action roles, instead of just playing the male hero's girlfriend or sidekick. Prime examples of the new women-led action series were *Charlie's Angels*, starring Farah Fawcett Majors, and *Wonder Woman*, with Linda Carter.

Crazy humour was in vogue, with the Monty Python team in Britain and the spoof series *Soap* in the USA. Nostalgia for more secure, stable times was evident in programmes such as *Upstairs Downstairs* and *The Waltons. Happy Days*, with Henry Winkler as The Fonz, played on nostalgia for the pre-Beatles youth era. *The Muppets* was the top children's programme, making stars of Kermit the Frog and Miss Piggy.

Changing times

In the 1970s, young people began to collect music on cassettes as well as vinyl discs. In 1979, the Sony Walkman was marketed as the first personal stereo. Young people also had video games to play for the first time. These were primitive and two-dimensional. The two players batted a spot of light back and forth, pretending that this was tennis, soccer or hockey. Skateboards were 'in' in a big way, and rollerskates were back – far more sophisticated than the ones enjoyed by earlier generations.

▽ *Skateboarding really took off in the 1970s.*

More activities were provided for children in the 1970s. For example, Disney World was created in Florida in 1971, and many smaller 'theme parks' opened. The expanding chains of fast-food restaurants, most notably McDonalds, were extremely 'child-friendly'. Some adults complained that childhood was being commercialized, but this really meant that there was more for children to own and do.

Date list

1970

17 April ▷ The Apollo 13 spacecraft arrives safely back on Earth, after an explosion in space brings its Moon flight abruptly to an end.

22 April ▷ Millions of Americans mark Earth Day, to raise awareness of ecological problems.

4 May ▷ National Guardsmen shoot dead four young anti-war protesters at Kent State University, Ohio.

21 June ▷ Brazil win the football World Cup, defeating Italy 4-1 in the final.

18 September ▷ Rock superstar Jimi Hendrix dies in London.

1971

26 March ▷ Bangladesh declares itself independent of Pakistan.

30 June ▷ The voting age in the USA is lowered from 21 to 18.

Also in 1971 ... ▷ Silicon chips are introduced, the beginning of the computer revolution.

1972

30 January ▷ On 'Bloody Sunday', 13 Northern Ireland Catholics are shot dead by British paratroopers in Londonderry.

21 February ▷ Richard Nixon visits communist China, the first US president to do so.

1 September ▷ Bobby Fischer becomes world chess champion, defeating Boris Spassky.

5 September ▷ Eleven members of the Israeli Olympic squad die in a Palestinian terrorist attack at the Munich games.

1973

1 January ▷ Britain, Ireland and Denmark join the European Community.

22 January ▷ A US Supreme Court judgement in the case of Roe v Wade makes abortion legal throughout the USA.

27 February ▷ Native American radicals begin an armed protest at the Sioux reservation of Wounded Knee.

29 March ▷ The last US troops leave South Vietnam.

6 October ▷ Egypt attacks Israeli forces along the Suez Canal, starting the Yom Kippur War. The war leads to a massive rise in world oil prices.

13 December ▷ British Prime Minister Edward Heath declares a 'three-day week' in industry to conserve fuel in the face of a threatened strike by coalminers.

1974

4 February ▷ American heiress Patty Hearst is kidnapped by the Symbionese Liberation Front, a revolutionary group. She eventually takes part in armed raids organized by her kidnappers.

13 February ▷ Russian dissident author Aleksandr Solzhenitsyn is deported from the Soviet Union to the West.

9 August ▷ President Nixon resigns to avoid impeachment over his part in a cover-up after the 1972 break-in at the Watergate building in Washington DC.

12 September ▷ Ethiopian Emperor Haile Selassie is overthrown and replaced by a left-wing military government.

29 October ▷ In a championship bout in Zaire, boxer Muhammad Ali knocks out George Foreman to regain the world heavyweight title he held in the 1960s.

21 November ▷ IRA bombs kill 21 people in two pubs in Birmingham.

1975

1 January ▷ The first International Women's Year begins.

30 April ▷ Communist forces capture Saigon, the capital of South Vietnam.

18 June ▷ The first oil is pumped ashore from oilfields under the North Sea.

5 July ▷ African American tennis player Arthur Ashe wins the Wimbledon men's singles.

15 July ▷ US and Soviet astronauts meet in space.

11 November ▷ The African state of Angola becomes independent of Portugal, but is immediately plunged into civil war.

20 November ▷ General Franco, dictator of Spain since the 1930s, dies. King Juan Carlos becomes ruler of Spain and soon introduces democracy.

Also in 1975 … ▷ The first personal computer (PC) goes on sale in the USA.

1976

4 July ▷ Americans celebrate the Bicentennial, the 200th anniversary of the American Declaration of Independence.

20 July ▷ The Viking 1 spacecraft lands on Mars.

28 July ▷ At least 242,000 people are killed as an earthquake destroys the Chinese city of Tangshan.

9 September ▷ Mao Tse-tung, the communist ruler of China since 1949, dies.

2 November ▷ Democrat Jimmy Carter is elected president of the USA.

1977

17 January ▷ Gary Gilmore is executed, the first person to suffer the death penalty in the USA for 10 years.

27 March ▷ The world's worst air disaster takes place at Tenerife in the Canary Islands. Two jumbo jets collide on the ground, killing 583 people.

Also in 1977 … ▷ Punk rock music and styles are at their peak in Britain.

1978

9 May ▷ Italian political leader Aldo Moro is murdered by terrorists of the Red Brigades.

25 July ▷ The world's first test-tube baby, Louise Brown, is born in Oldham.

17 September ▷ The Camp David accord lays the foundation for peace between Egypt and Israel.

16 October ▷ Polish archbishop Karol Wojtyla is elected pope, taking the name John Paul II.

1979

16 January ▷ The Shah of Iran flees into exile, overthrown in an Islamic Revolution inspired by the Ayatollah Khomeini.

28 March ▷ A serious accident occurs at the Three Mile Island nuclear power station in Pennsylvania.

4 June ▷ Conservative leader Margaret Thatcher becomes Britain's first woman prime minister, ending five years of Labour government.

19 July ▷ A revolution in Nicaragua overthrows the dictator Anastasio Somoza and brings the left-wing Sandinistas to power.

21 December ▷ A peace deal ends the illegal independence of white-ruled Rhodesia. It will become legally independent as black-ruled Zimbabwe.

Glossary

aborigines

The original inhabitants of Australia who were there when the Europeans arrived in the 1700s.

aerobics

Fast exercises designed to increase fitness by making the body consume more oxygen.

American Indian Movement

A group of Native Americans who fought for improved civil rights.

ayatollah

A religious leader among the Shi'ite Muslims, especially in Iran.

Baader Meinhof gang

A West German left-wing terrorist movement, also known as the Red Army Faction (RAF).

bellbottoms

Trousers or jeans that get much wider below the knee.

blaxploitation

This term was made up from the words 'black' and 'exploitation' to describe action movies of the 1970s aimed at an African American audience.

blockbuster

This was originally a term for a powerful bomb capable of knocking down a whole row of buildings. It is now used for a big-budget movie designed to pull in the largest possible audiences.

boat people

Refugees who fled from communist-ruled Vietnam by sea in the late 1970s.

bussing

Sending children from predominantly white districts of American cities to schools in predominantly black districts, and vice versa, in order to achieve mixed-race education.

CAT scan

CAT stands for computed axial tomography – a way of building up a three-dimensional X-ray image of the inside of the body.

dashiki

A type of loose shirt, originally worn mostly in Africa.

dissident

People who protested against oppression and censorship in the Soviet Union were known as dissidents.

FBI

FBI stands for Federal Bureau of Investigation. The FBI is the police force responsible for enforcing federal laws in the USA.

Gay Liberation

A movement campaigning for an end to prejudice against homosexuals.

impeachment

Under the US constitution, the House of

Representatives can charge the US president with a criminal offence. This is called impeachment. If impeached, the president is tried by the Senate.

Inuit

The Inuit people live in Canada, Greenland and Alaska. They were once known as Eskimos.

IRA

IRA stands for Irish Republican Army, a terrorist movement that has fought to end British rule in Northern Ireland.

Islamic fundamentalists

Muslims who believe in a return to strict Islamic law and customs.

militants

People who are actively committed to a political cause and are sometimes prepared to use violence in their political struggle.

NMR scan

NMR stand for Nuclear Magnetic Resonance. NMR scans give a picture of what is happening inside the body.

oil sheikh

A sheikh is an Arab chieftain. When some Arab rulers became rich through the discovery of petroleum on their land, they were jokingly called 'oil sheikhs'.

postmodernism

Postmodernism is a term used for many different kinds of art and architecture that reacted against the modernism of the first half of the 20th century.

Red Brigades

Left-wing terrorists who carried out kidnappings and assassinations in Italy in the 1970s.

skijack

A word made up from 'sky' and 'hijack' to describe the hijacking of an airliner.

space probe

A spacecraft designed to voyage far from the Earth and send back information about the places to which it travels.

stadium band

A rock band that had become so popular or grandiose that it could only perform in a large stadium.

street funk

An earthy African American music of the early 1970s blending the influence of jazz and soul music.

supergroup

An all-star rock band formed by well-known performers from different groups getting together. Examples of supergroups included Crosby, Stills, Nash and Young, and Emerson, Lake and Palmer.

teenybopper

A term invented in the 1970s for early teenage pop fans.

tie-dye

A method for hand-dyeing fabrics in a coloured pattern. The pattern is produced by tying knots in the cloth before it is put in the dye.

Resources

Books

Rolling Stone: The Seventies, published in 1998, is a lavish and entertaining look at many 1970s fads and issues, written by people who were there.

The Virgin Encyclopedia of Seventies Music is a comprehensive reference, from Abba to Zappa.

The 1970s started with the publication of two feminist classics, *Sexual Politics* by Kate Millett and Germaine Greer's *The Female Eunuch*. Reading these decidedly adult books takes you to the roots of the 1970s women's movement.

An easier read is Marilyn French's feminist novel *The Women's Room*, one of the '70s' biggest sellers.

John Irving's best-seller *The World According to Garp* is partly a male answer to the more extreme forms of 1970s feminism.

Tales of the City by American novelist Armistead Maupin is a classic that expresses the feel-good side of the decade.

Written in the 1990s, *Bad Haircut* by Tom Perrotta is an amusing set of tales about adolescence in New Jersey in the 1970s.

Hanif Kureishi's novel *The Buddha of Suburbia* looks back affectionately at growing up in '70s London.

On a lighter note, *Mad about the Seventies: The Best of the Decade* is a compilation of excerpts from *Mad* magazine providing a hilarious take on the times.

If you can find them, the Fabulous Furry Freak Brothers comic strips, starring Fat Freddy's Cat, give a side-splitting taste of the anarchy of the early 1970s post-Hippie world.

Internet

Going to www.yahoo.com and typing in Seventies in the search box is the gateway to a treasure-trove of varied material on the decade.

Music

You could arrange a fascinating musical trip for yourself through a fast-changing decade, starting with heavy metal band Led Zeppelin, moving through the arty period of Pink Floyd's *Dark Side of the Moon* and David Bowie's *Ziggy Stardust* to the raw aggression of the Sex Pistols and the Clash, and on to Elvis Costello's New Wave album *This Year's Model*. Or instead you could choose the Osmonds, Abba, the Bee Gees, YMCA …

Art and architecture

Seventies architecture is worth a visit if you have a chance to travel to the Opera House in Sydney or the Pompidou Centre in Paris.

Much of the art of the time, including Christo's works, was not built to last and no longer exists.

Ransack your parents' old record collection for album covers of the period.

Films

Many of the key movies of the 1970s were obsessed with sex and/or violence, so in principle you are not allowed to watch them. However, many of the best films of the decade are often shown on television and worth seeing.

For the rebellious, anti-authority side of the 1970s, try *One Flew Over the Cuckoo's Nest*, starring Jack Nicholson, or *Dog Day Afternoon* with Al Pacino.

Alice Doesn't Live Here Any More, starring Ellen Burstyn, is a good example of 1970s feminism.

Shaft is a classic 'blaxploitation' movie.

Little Big Man, starring Dustin Hoffman and made in 1971, shows the new attitude to Native Americans. In a complete reversal of the once popular 'cowboys and Indians' movies, the Cheyenne are the good guys opposed to the brutal whites.

The growing opposition to nuclear power in the 1970s found expression in *The China Syndrome*, starring Jane Fonda and released in 1979, the same year as the Three Mile Island disaster.

Meryl Streep played Karen Silkwood (see page 16) in the 1980s movie *Silkwood*.

All The President's Men is a movie about the start of the Watergate affair (see page 6) made soon after the event.

The 1990s movie *Nixon*, starring Anthony Hopkins, is also worth seeing.

The Killing Fields, made in the 1980s, gives a good impression of what happened in Cambodia under Pol Pot (see page 8).

In *Saturday Night Fever* and *Grease* you can experience the excitement of the 1970s disco boom at first hand.

The 1975 movie *Tommy*, built around music by the Who, is an impressive example of the kind of pretentious rock that punk rebelled against.

If you can get to see it, *The Great Rock'n'Roll Swindle*, starring Malcolm Maclaren and the Sex Pistols and made in 1979, is a direct expression of punk.

Quotations

The quotations in this book are from the following sources: Page 4: Hilary Kingsley and Geoff Tibballs, *Box of Delights, The Golden Years of Television*, Macmillan, 1989; Page 8: *The Listener*, 15 February 1979; Page 12: E. F. Schumacher, *Small is Beautiful*, 1973; Page 15: Barry Commoner, *The Closing Circle*, 1971, quoted in Arthur Marwick, *The Sixties*, Oxford University Press, 1998; Pages 18 and 19: Valerie Steele, *Fifty Years of Fashion*, Yale University Press, 1993; Pages 24 and 25: *The NME Rock'n'Roll Years*, Hamlyn, 1992; Page 32:Godfrey Hodgson, *People's 20th Century, From the start of the nuclear age to the end of the century*, BBC Books, 1996; Page 36: Jonathon Green, *The Pan Dictionary of Contemporary Quotations*, Pan, 1989.

Index